Dear Parents and Educators,

The Learnalots™ were created for kids, but we think you will love them too! They deliver important educational content through fun and engaging activities.

The Learnalots are mascots for learning eight essential subjects, as defined by national early learning standards. Each of the Learnalots represent one specific subject. We place special emphasis on math and literacy, since they are fundamental to academic success. We have also included activities in science, creative arts, music, social skills, health and fitness, and nature.

We are dedicated to ensuring that our products provide a broad and rich learning experience for young children. Building a child's confidence and enthusiasm for learning at an early age is critical to future success. It is our sincere hope that the Learnalots will inspire children, and those who care for them, to learn something new everyday.

~ The BrightStart Learning Team

Thank You for making us part of your child's early learning experience. We welcome your thoughts and feedback. You can reach us at: info@brightstartlearning.com

A a

Learn about letters by first **tracing** the outlines.
Then practice **writing** the letter on your own.

Anteater

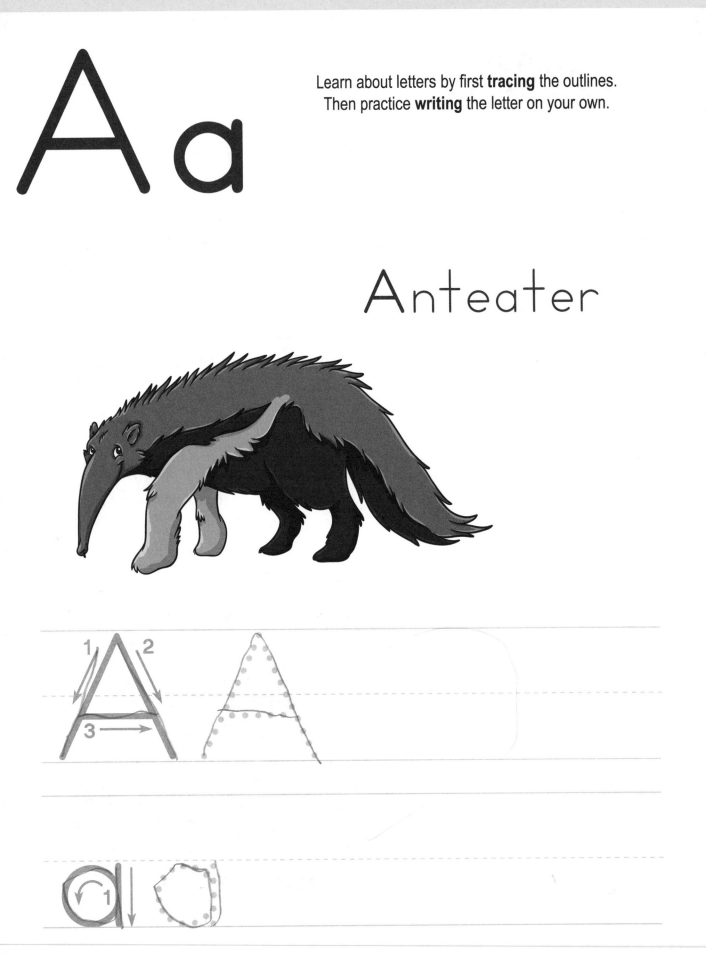

The Letter Aa

ant

apple

airplanes

Bb

Bird

The Learnalots

The Letter Bb

bell

ball

butterfly

Cc

Camel

The Learnalots

The Letter Cc

cat car

clock coat

Dd

Dolphin

The Learnalots™

The Letter Dd

drum

dog

duck

dress

E e

Eagle

The Learnalots™

The Letter E e

elk

ear

eye

earth

F f

Fox

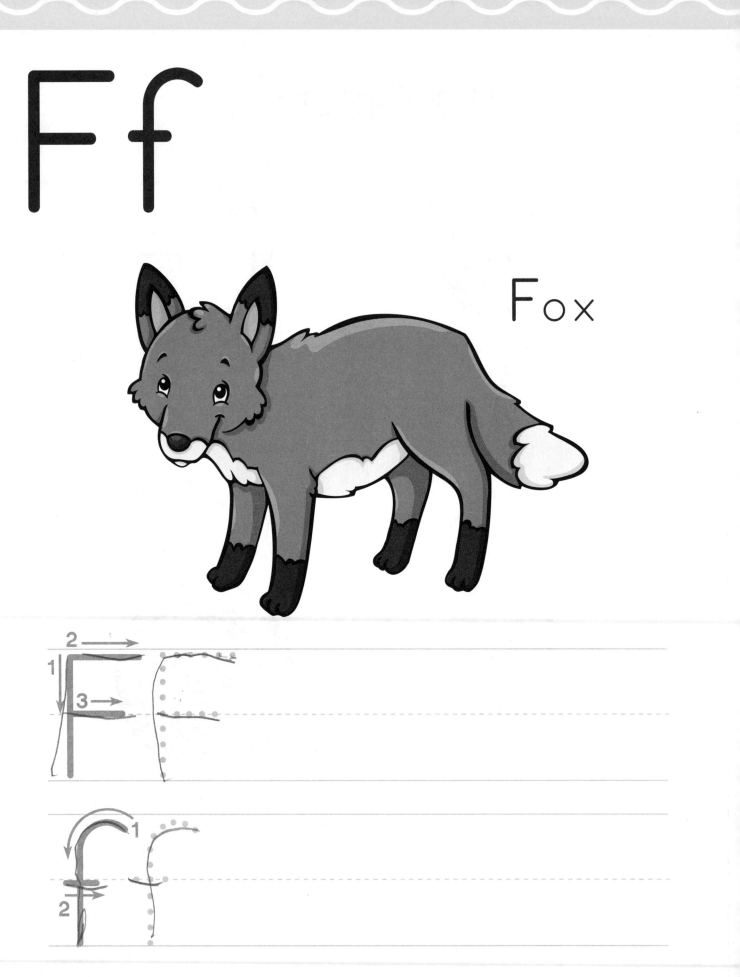

The Learnalots

The Letter F f

fish   frog

flowers

Gg

Goat

The Learnalots

The Letter Gg

gift   ghost

grapes

Hh

Hedgehog

The Learnalots

The Letter Hh

hat

harp

hive

heart

I i

Iguana

The Learnalots

The Letter Ii

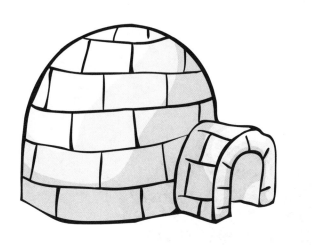 

gloo   ron

ce cream

Jj

Jaguar

2 →
1
J

1
2
j

The Learnalots™

The Letter Jj

jelly

jeep

jellyfish

K k

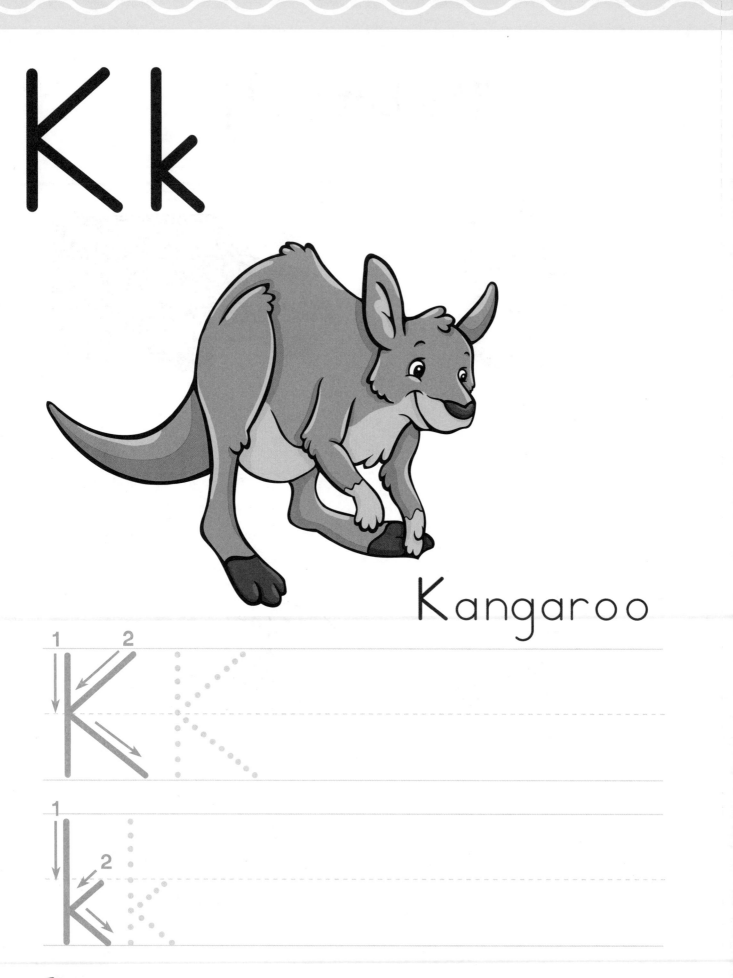

Kangaroo

The Letter Kk

key

kitty

kite

koala

Ll

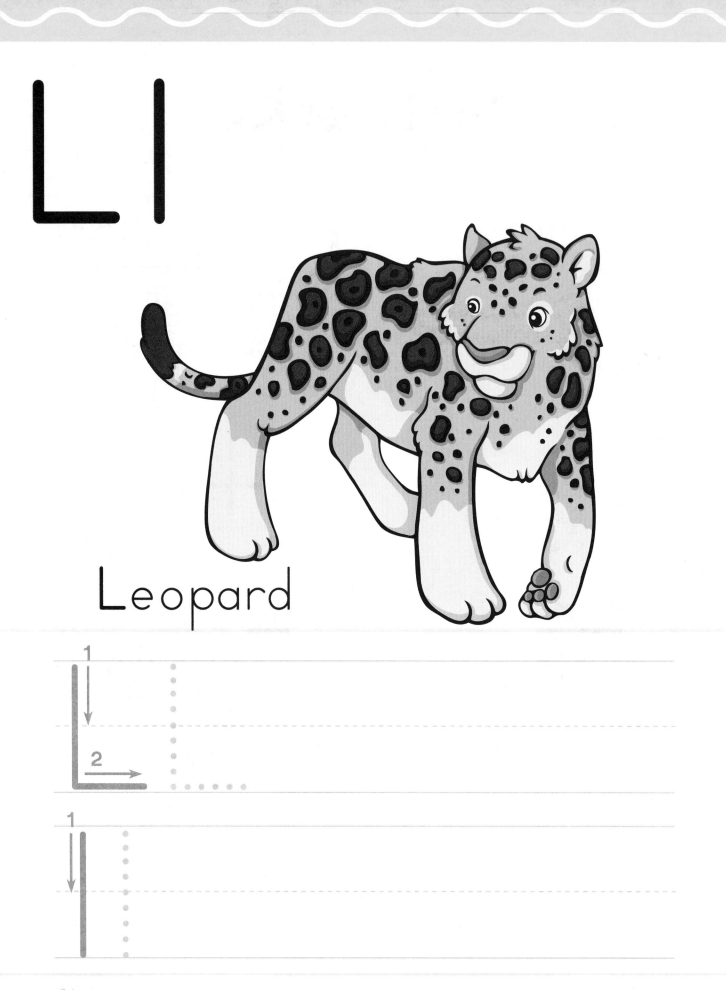

Leopard

The Learnalots

The Letter L l

emon og

ock eaf

Mm

Mouse

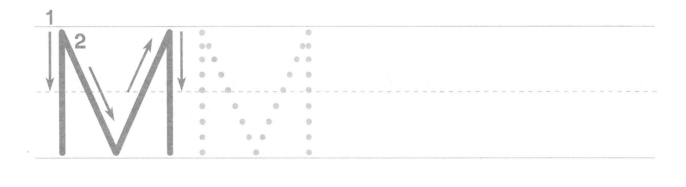

The Learnalots™

The Letter Mm

milk

moon

mittens

N n

Nuthatch

The Learnalots

The Letter N n

nest   nut

necklace

O o

O w l

The Learnalots

The Letter Oo

oar

olive

octopus

P p

Pig

The Learnalots

The Letter Pp

paw   piano

pumpkins

Qq

Quail

The Learnalots

The Letter Qq

quill   quilt

queen

Rr

Rabbit

The Learnalots

The Letter Rr

rain　ring

rockets

S s

Skunk

The Learnalots

The Letter Ss

now   eal

ocks   oup

T t

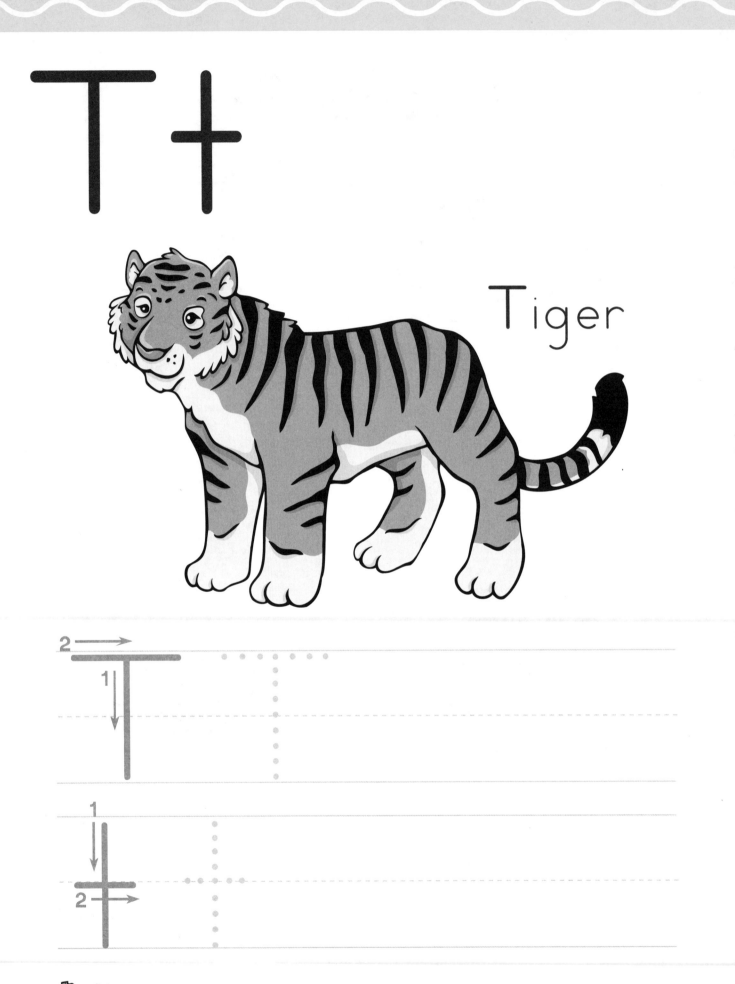

Tiger

The Learnalots

The Letter T t

ree

oys

adpoles

U u

Urial

The Letter U u

umbrellas

V v

Vole

The Learnalots

The Letter V v

violin

volcano

W w

Whale

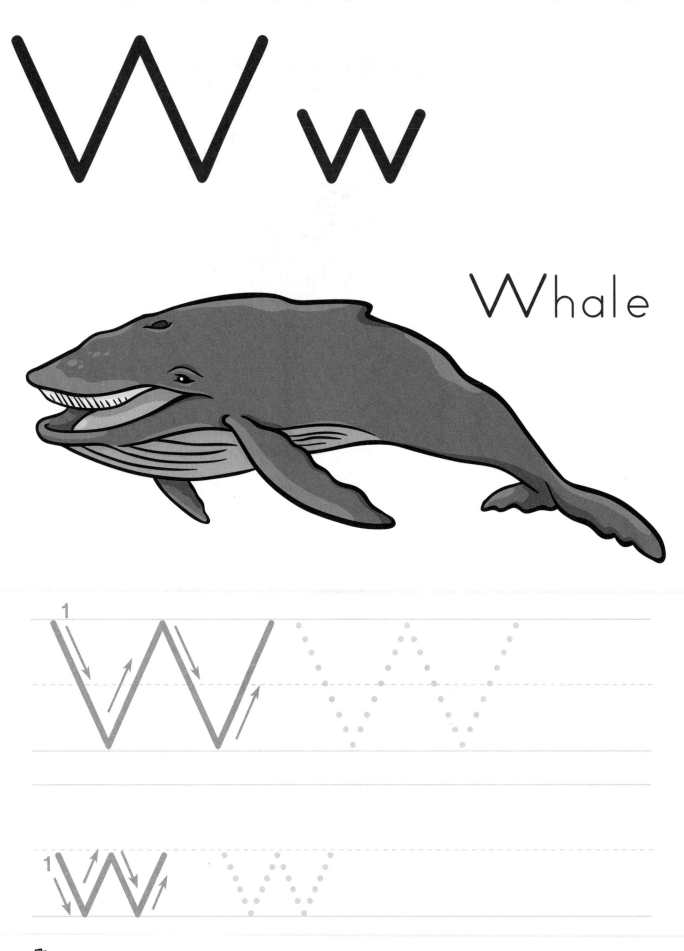

The Learnalots

The Letter W w

well wolf

worms

X x

X-ray fish

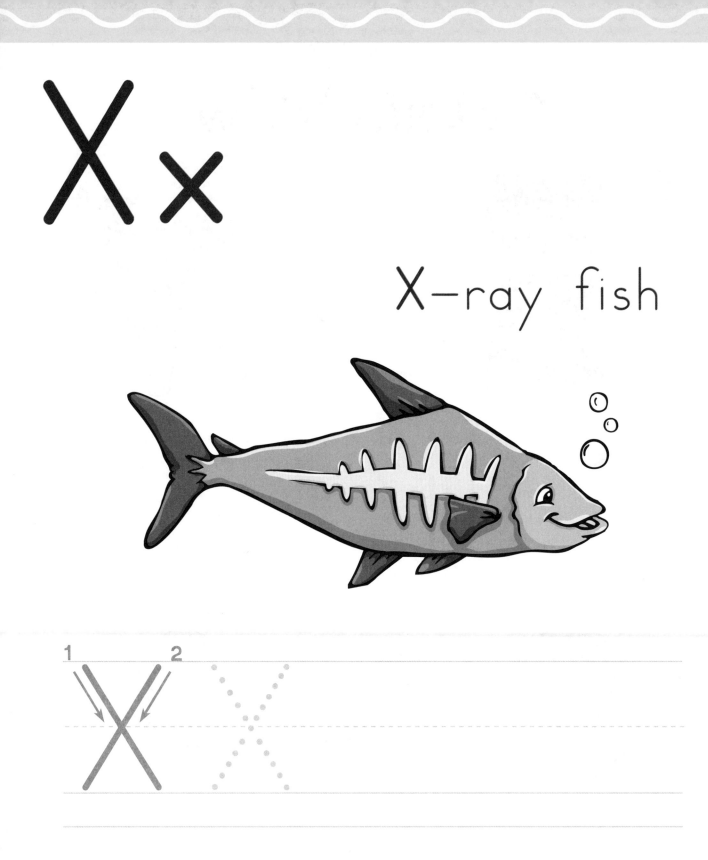

The Letter Xx

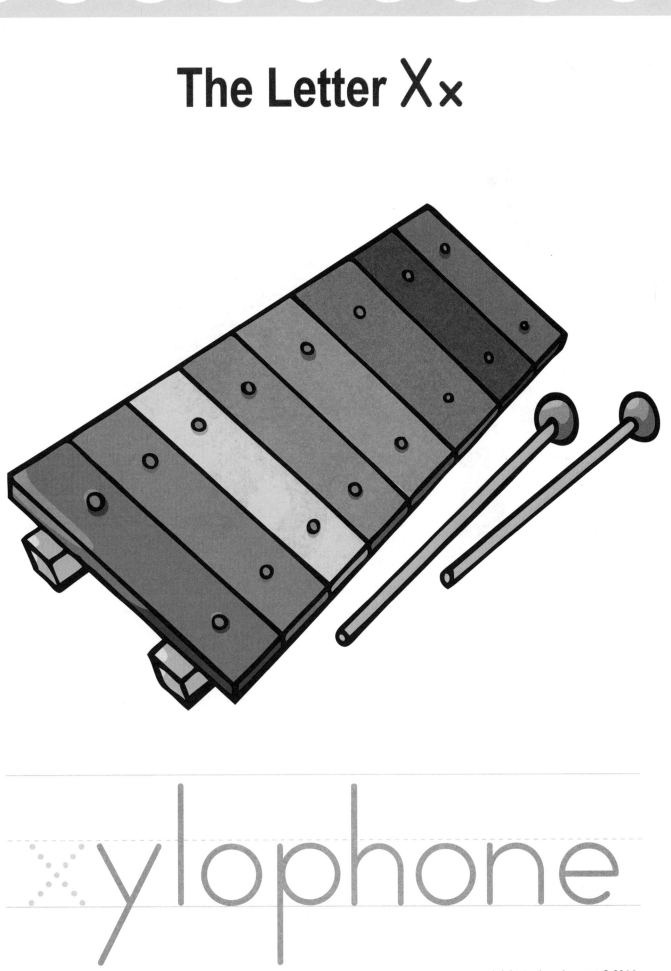

xylophone

Y y

Yak

The Learnalots™

The Letter Yy

yarn

yo-yo

yogurt

Z z

Zebra

The Learnalots

The Letter Zz

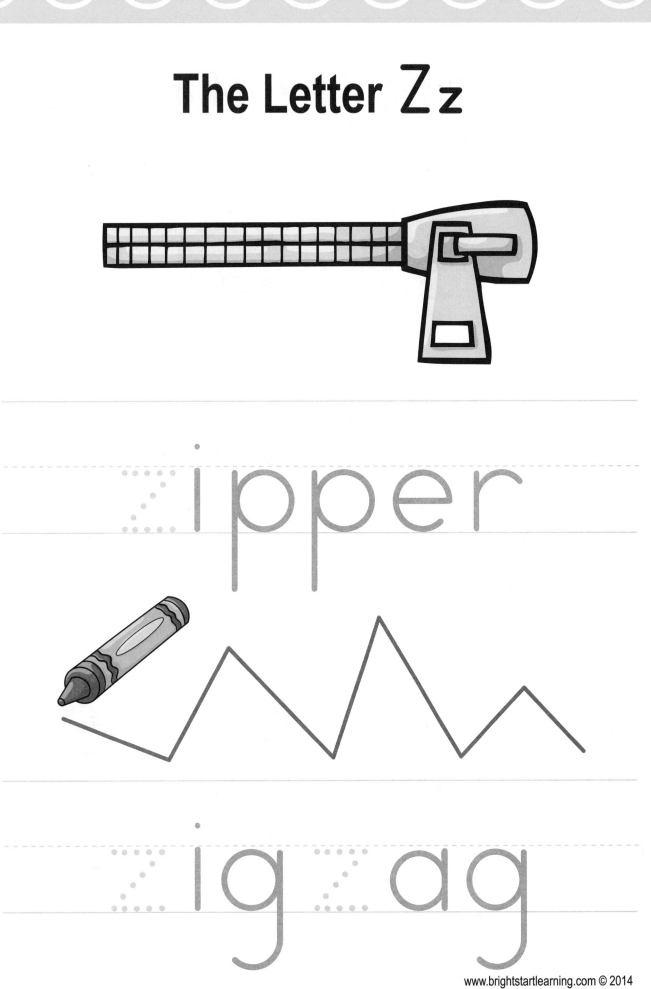

zipper

zigzag

Tracing the Alphabet

Trace each dotted letter to write the alphabet.

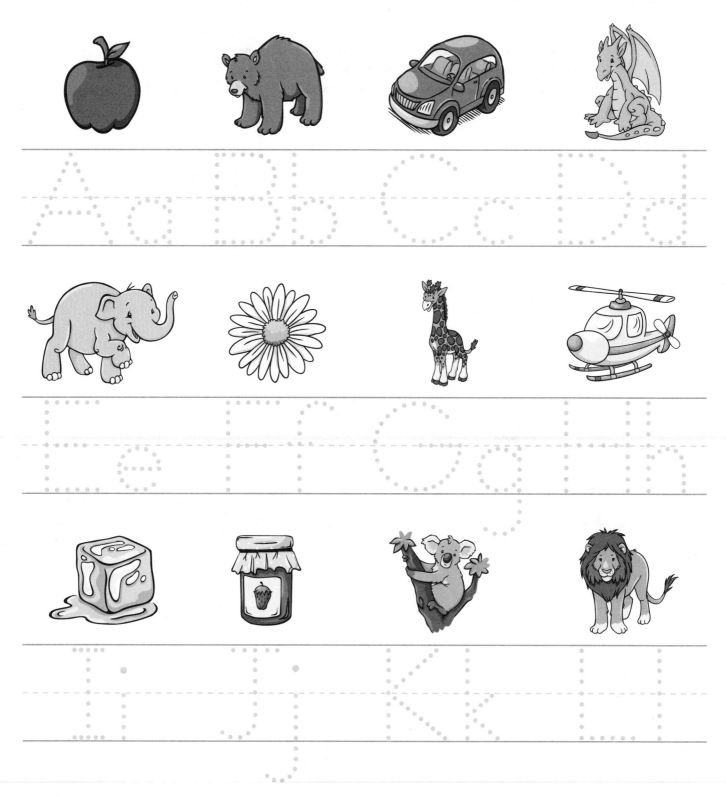

The Learnalots

Find the "P's"

P is for Puppy.
Follow the pictures that begin with P to **find** the puppy's brothers and sisters.

Vacation Information

Write your name, address, and phone number on this luggage tag before your trip!

Name: _____

Address: _____

_____

Phone Number: _____

Which Doesn't Rhyme?

In each group of pictures, one doesn't rhyme. **Cross out** the picture that doesn't rhyme.

The Learnalots™

Chalkboard Words

Help Bo **find** the words on this chalkboard and **circle** them.

jelly   drum   flower   ladybug   cat

c v d r w o t d g x r
a d j q f l o w e r u
j e r s n z c b a
e i f u c o a v
l a b z m g t
l a d y b u g
y n p x e k c

The Learnalots

Letter Matching

Circle the letter that each picture begins with.

A C S R

B T V P

I O Q Y

H M U W

Scrambled Letters

These letters are mixed up!
Put these letters in alphabetical order by **writing** them on the lines.

CED

SQR

The Learnalots

Letter Styles

Letters sometimes look different when they are written by hand or printed by a computer.
How many letter A's or a's can you find? **Write** the number in the box.

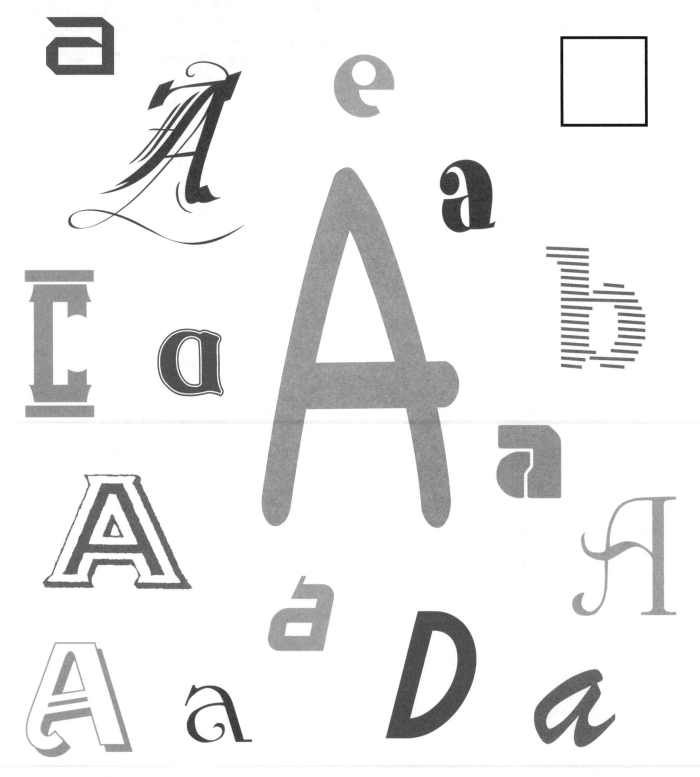

The Learnalots

Vowel Words

Draw a line to connect each picture with its beginning letter.

a

e

i

o

u

Days of the Week

Trace the word for each day of the week. Then **write** each word on the line below it.

The Learnalots™

Thursday

Friday

Saturday

Sunday

Tic-Tac-Toe with Letters

Play tic-tac-toe! **Cross out** the pictures in each board that begins with the letter next to it.
Three in a row wins!

The Learnalots

T

W

X Marks the Spot

Follow the path of X's to **find** the treasure chest!

V	X	A	B	X	X	X
X	X	X	X	X	C	X
X	M	O	X	Q	L	X
X	W	X	S	Z	X	X
X	X	X	D	T	X	R

The Learnalots

Rhyming with Stickers

Add stickers to match the shaded images.
Then, **draw a line** to connect each rhyming pair.

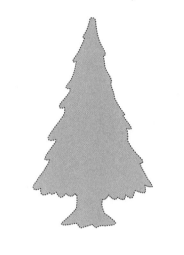

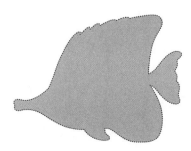

Up in the Sky

Help Leo learn the names of these sky objects. Practice **tracing** the words.

sun

moon

planet

The Learnalots™

cloud

star

rocket

Pathways

Trace the pathway taken by each object.

The Learnalots

Land, Water, or Air?

Vehicles can travel on land, water, or through the air. **Circle** the vehicles that travel on water.

Star Pictures

Stars in the night sky make pictures called constellations.
Draw a line to connect each constellation to the animal you think it looks like.

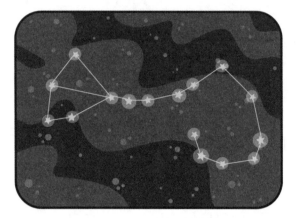

Ursa Major (Big Bear)

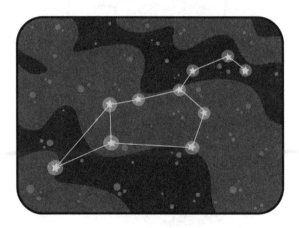

Scorpio the Scorpion

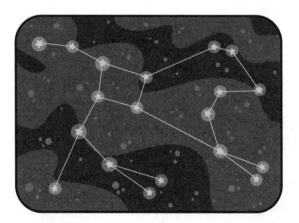

Leo the Lion

The Learnalots

Scared Animals

When scared, some animals defend themselves by puffing up, hiding, or using spines.
Draw a line to connect each normal and scared animal.

Natural Wonders

Help put the science objects away.
Draw a line from the backpack to the objects that are **made by people**.
Draw a line from the box to the objects **from nature**.

Science Tools

Nature Objects

Living or Not?

Some things are living, some things are not. **Circle** the living things.

Volcanoes!

The volcano is erupting! **Write** the numbers **1, 2, 3, and 4** to order the pictures.

The Learnalots

Solids, Liquids, or Gases

Objects can be solids, liquids, or gases.
Draw a line between each object and the word that describes its state.

Solid   **Liquid**   **Gas**

Snowy Weather

Circle the clothes that will keep you warm on a snowy day.

The Learnalots

Hot and Cold

We use thermometers to measure temperature. When the temperature is high it is warm out, and when the temperature is low it is cold out. **Circle** the correct thermometer for each object.

Snow Symmetry

Draw a line to connect each snowflake to its missing half.

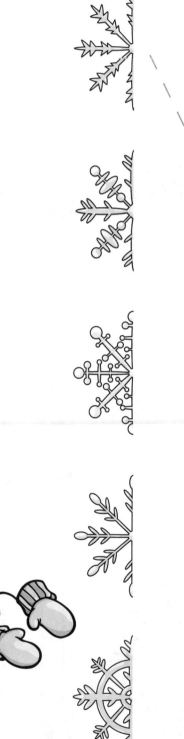

The Learnalots

Cloud Count

Help Leo **count** the clouds. **Write the number** in the box.

Quiet to Loud

All of these objects make noise.
Write 1 next to the quietest noise, 3 next to the loudest noise, and 2 for the noise that is in between.

The Learnalots

5 Senses

We have five senses: sight, smell, taste, touch and hear.
Draw a line to connect each object with the sense you would use to explore it.

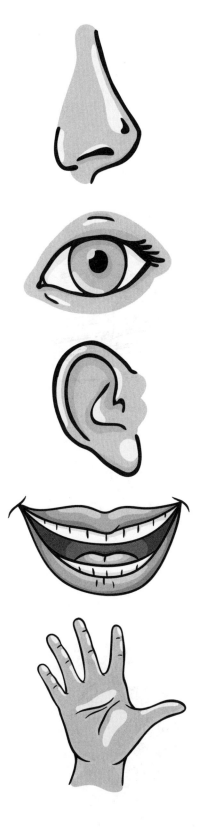

Float or Sink?

Some objects float in water and some sink. **Circle** the objects that float.

Electric Tools

Some objects need electricity to work. **Cross out** the objects that don't need electricity.

Science Tools

There are many different tools that can be used in science.
Circle the tools on both pages you might be able to use to study science.

The Learnalots

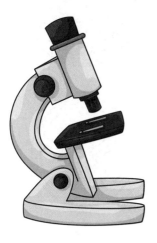

Healthy Patterns

Fruits and vegetables have patterns inside them. **Draw a line** to match the insides to the outsides.

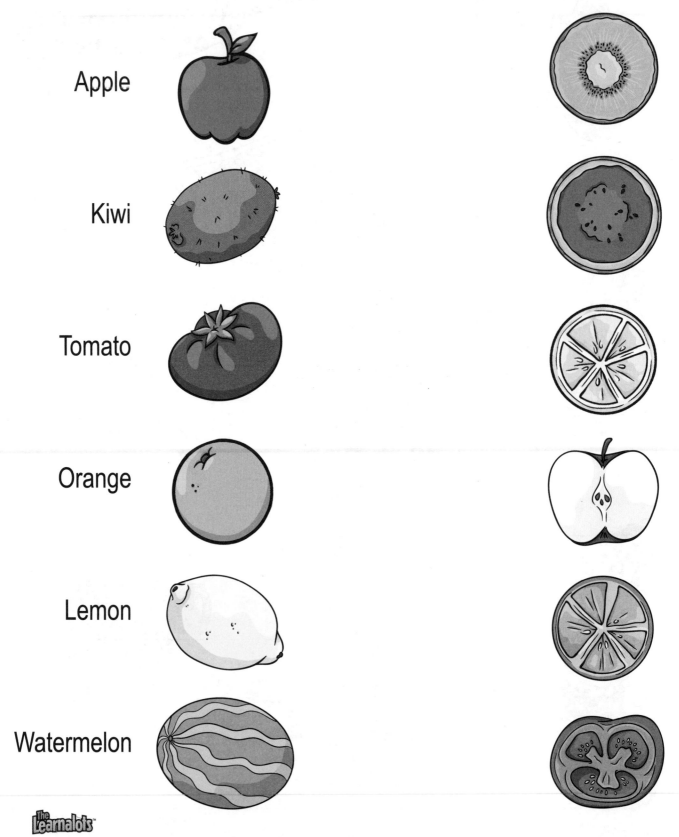

Apple

Kiwi

Tomato

Orange

Lemon

Watermelon

The Learnalots™

Star Search

What does Leo see? **Fill** the night sky with space stickers.

Art Supplies

In each row, two objects are used to make art. **Cross out** the object that doesn't belong.

The Learnalots

Doodle Sub

Make these mini-subs look the same by **drawing** what is missing.

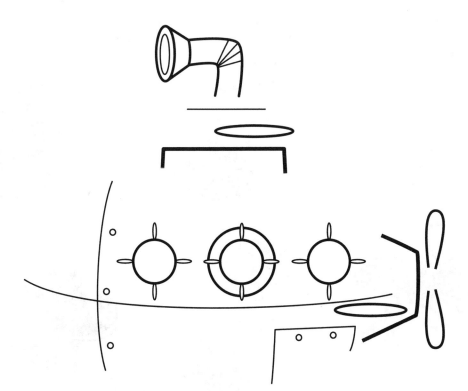

Inky Insects

Draw a line to connect each insect with its matching color.

Color Garden

Read the color words. Then, **color** the flowers.

Pink

Red

Orange

Green

Yellow

Blue

Alien Space Travel

Make believe! **Connect the dots**, 1-21, and color the alien and U.F.O.

The Learnalots™

Whoo Goes There?

Whoo, whoo! **Draw** the owl's face, then **color** it.

Rainy Day Match

Draw a line to connect the rain boots and their matching umbrellas.

The Learnalots

Step-by-Step Frog Sketch

Follow the steps to **draw** a frog in the empty box.

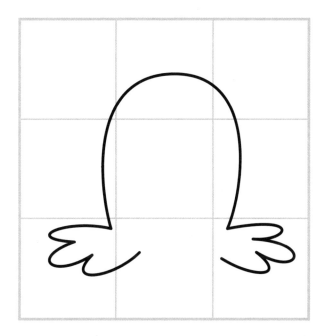

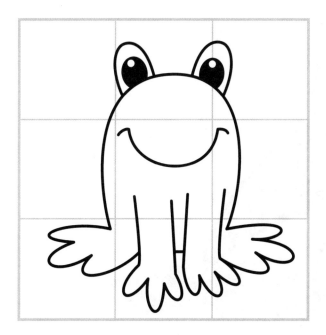

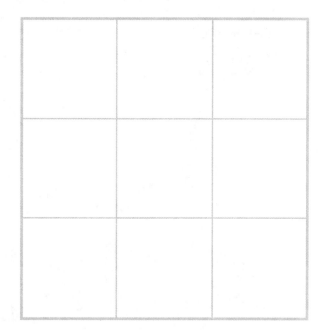

Porcupine Portrait

This porcupine is missing her quills! **Draw** the missing quills.

The Learnalots

Shapes & Colors

Red, yellow, and blue are primary colors.
Color the shapes using the colors shown below.

Egg Match

Put the Easter eggs back together. **Draw** a line between the matching pieces.

The Learnalots

Bulldozer Doodle

Make these bulldozers look the same by **drawing** the **missing parts**. Then, **color** it!

Getting Warm!

Zak needs help coloring his fire.
Use **warm colors** like red, orange, and yellow to **color** the flames.

The Learnalots

Textures to the Touch

Draw a circle around the things that would feel **smooth**.
Draw a square around the things that would feel **rough**.

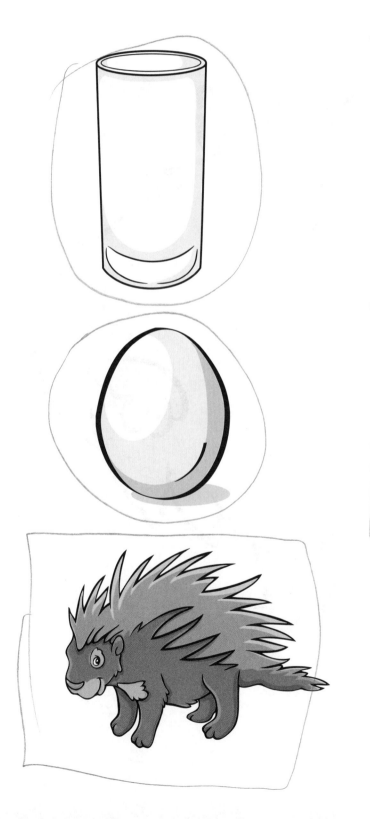

Monster Face

Draw a face on this monster and then **color** it!

The Learnalots™

Greedy Goat

Oh no! The goat ate the flowers. Can you fix it by **drawing** flowers on top of the stems?

Mixing Colors

Circle the color Zak will make by mixing together red and yellow clay.

The Learnalots™

Lion Doodle

Make these lions look the same by **drawing** the missing parts, then **color** it!

Pattern Splash

Cross out the swim trunks in each row that is different from the others.

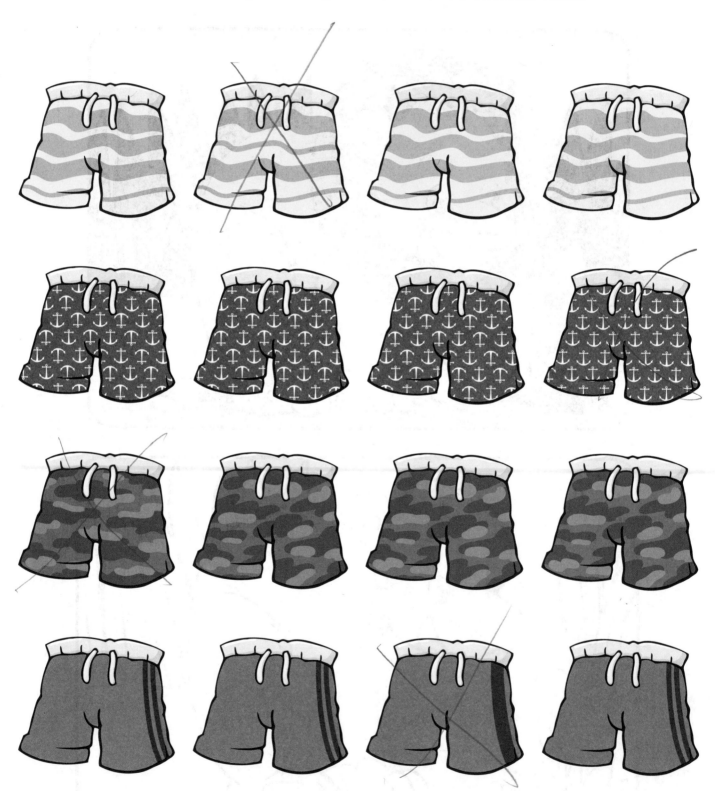

Step-by-Step Flower Sketch

Follow the steps to **draw** a flower in the empty box.

Artist's Toolbox

Draw a line to connect the artwork to the art supplies used to make it.

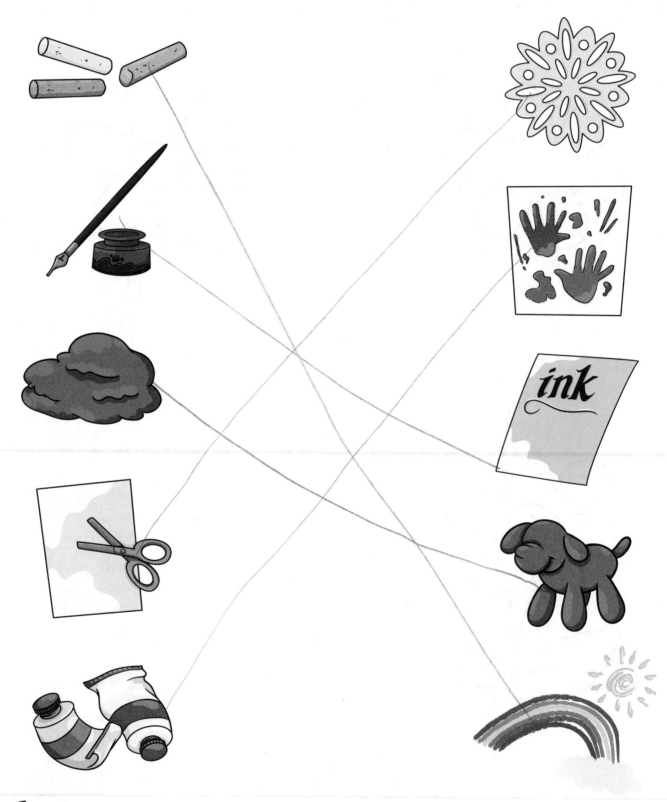

The Learnalots

Sparkle and Shine

Color the stones in the jewelry.

Grid Drawing: Hippo

Use the grid to help you **finish** the hippopotamus drawing.

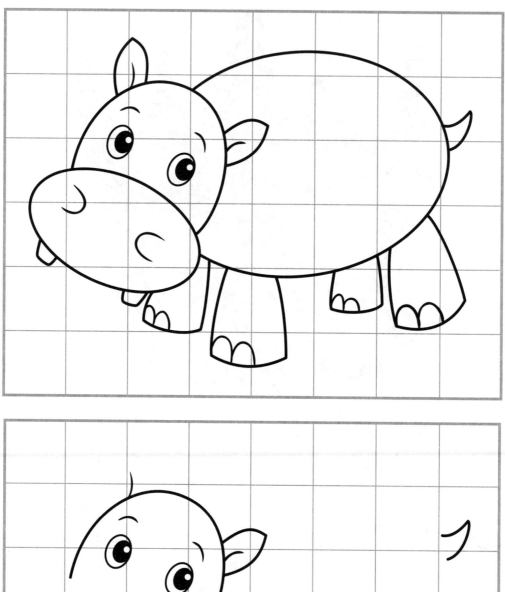

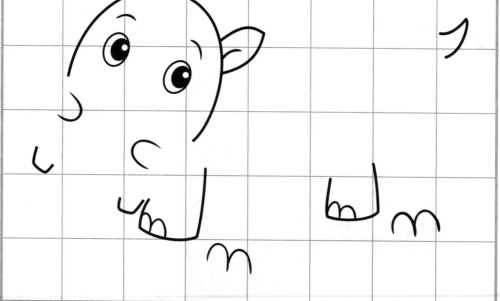

Scavenger Hunt

Help Zak **find** his painting.
Then, **add** art stickers to match the shaded images.

STICKER PAGE

START

Happy or Sad?

Draw a **smiley face** for the things that make you happy.
Draw a **sad face** for the things that make you sad.

The Learnalots™

Using Your Manners

Help Sofie make good choices at kindergarten.
Check the box for the picture that shows Sofie sharing with her friend.

The Learnalots

How Do I Feel?

Draw a line from each face to the word that describes how that person feels.

Happy   **Scared**   **Suprised**   **Angry**

My Family

Draw a picture of your family. Don't forget your pets!

The Learnalots™

Family Tree

Ask your parents to help you complete your family tree.
Draw pictures and **add** the names of people in your family. Put yourself on the top of the tree!

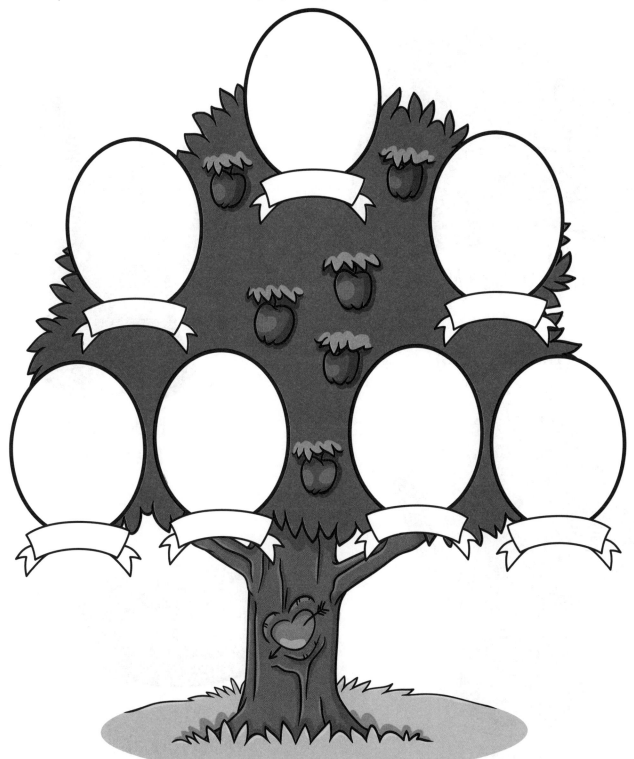

World Clothes

People around the world wear different clothing.
Circle the clothing on both pages you might like to try wearing.

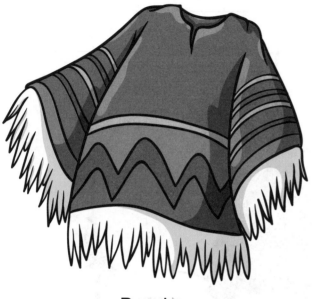

Poncho
(The Americas)

Lederhosen
(Germany)

Kimono
(Japan)

Kufi
(West Africa)

The Learnalots

Sari
(India)

Sombrero
(Mexico)

Grass Skirt
(Hawaii)

Parka
(The Arctic)

Clogs
(Netherlands)

Thank You!

There are many different ways to say thank you. **Trace** the words and **practice saying** these new words.

Gracias

Spanish

Arigato

Japanese

Obrigado

Portuguese

The Learnalots

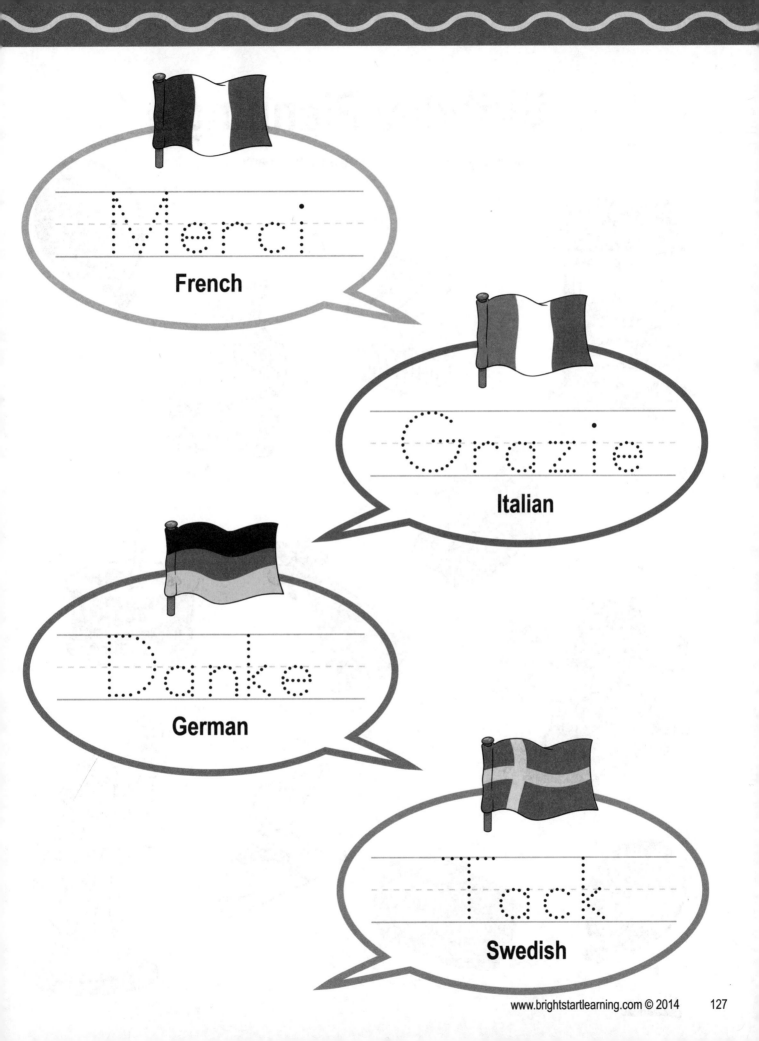

French

Italian

German

Swedish

Birthday Planning

Circle objects you would see at a birthday party.

The Learnalots

Valentine's Day

Valentine's Day is February 14th.
Can you **color** this valentine and **write** a message to someone special?

After You!

Look at the pictures on both pages. Sofie is opening doors for friends today.
Write the number in the box to match who Sofie is opening the door for.

Bo

1. Doll
2. Zak
3. Scout
4. Dog
5. Bo

Scout

Get Well Soon

Circle the items you would give to a friend who is feeling sick.

The Learnalots

Time to Play!

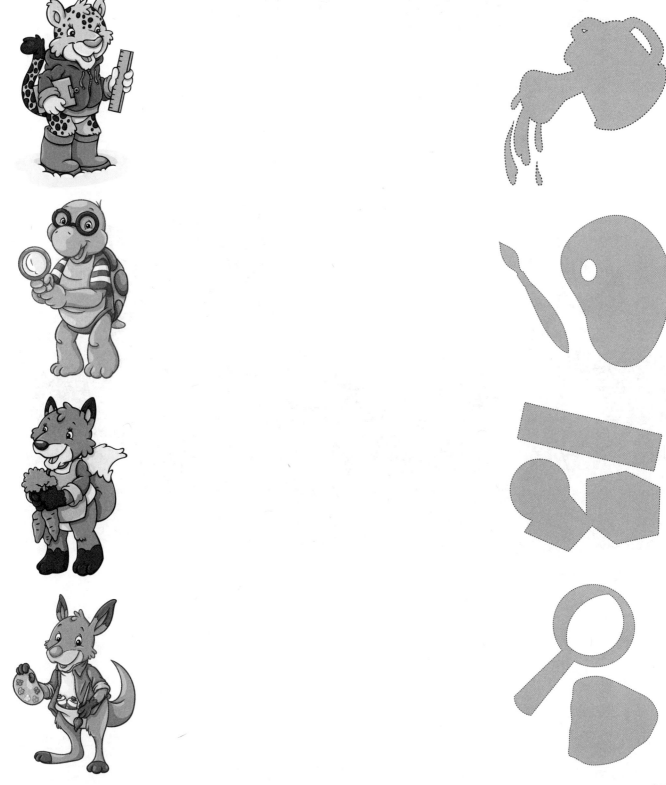

Add stickers to match the shaded images.
Then, draw a line to match each character with their favorite things.

STICKER PAGE

1 one hippo

one

The Learnalots

2 two
crocodiles

3 three zebras

three

three

4 four lions

four

The Learnalots

four

5 five monkeys

five

The Learnalots™

five

6 six birds

The Learnalots

six

7 seven snakes

seven

The Learnalots

seven

8 eight lizards

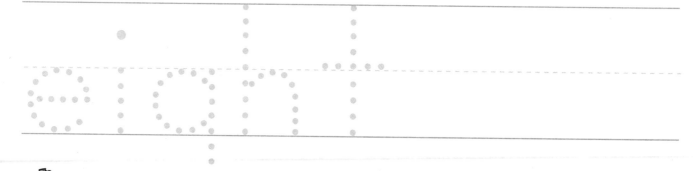

9 nine spiders

nine

The Learnalots™

nine

10 ten bees

The Learnalots

Numbers and Words

Trace each number and number word. Then **write** the number words on your own.

The Learnalots

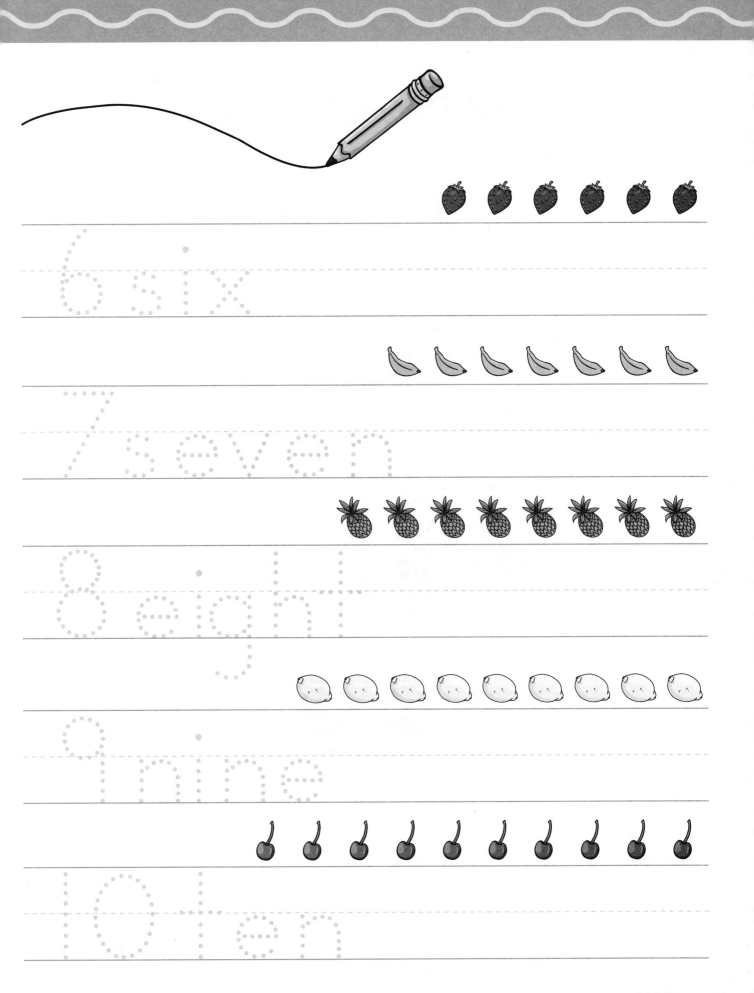

6 six

7 seven

8 eight

9 nine

10 ten

Robot Shapes

How many of each shape can you find? **Count** the shapes and **write** down the numbers in the boxes.

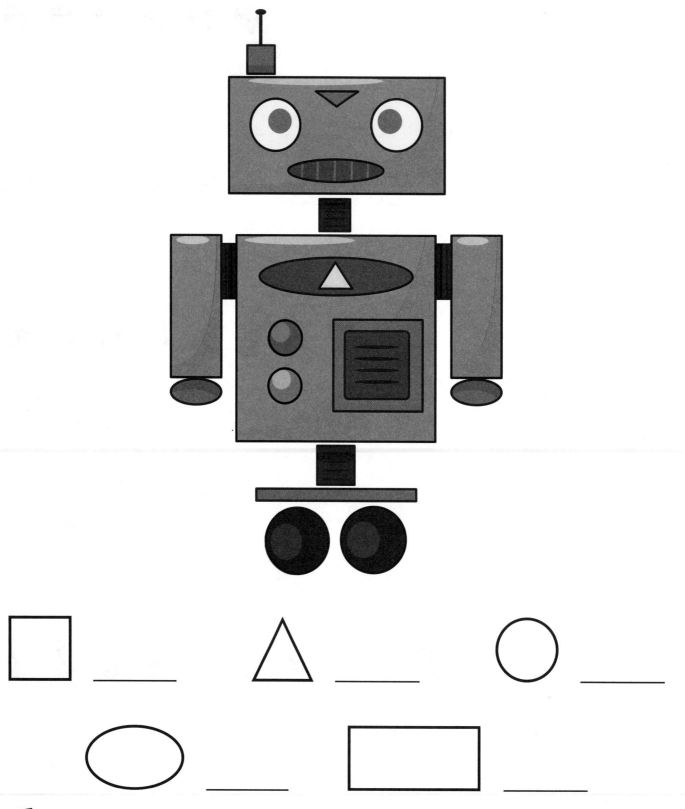

Learning Shapes

Trace each shape. **Fill in** each shape with a different color.

Rectangle

Diamond

Circle

Triangle

Octagon

Pattern Perfect!

Draw the shape that would come next in the pattern.

_____

_____

_____

The Learnalots

Which Wheels?

Draw a line from each vehicle to its missing wheel.

The Learnalots

Symmetry

Some of these pictures are symmetrical, which means they are the same on both sides of the dotted line. Others are asymmetrical, which means they aren't the same. **Circle** the pictures that are symmetrical.

Counting Caterpillars

How many caterpillars can you find in the garden?
Write the number in the box.

The Learnalots™

Number Snakes!

Fill in the blank spots on each snake with the correct number.

Missing Teeth

This shark is missing his teeth!
Draw 5 sharp teeth on the top and 5 sharp teeth on the bottom of his mouth.

The Learnalots™

All Buttoned Up!

Count the buttons on each raincoat. **Write** the number of buttons next to each raincoat.
Then, **circle** the coat that has the most buttons.

7

6

4

5

8

3

Fewer Toys

It's playtime for Kit and Leo!
Write down the number of each friend's toys.
Circle the name of the friend that has **FEWER** toys

Kit

The Learnalots

Leo

More Please!

Flora and Kit are having a picnic! **Write down** the number of each friend's food. **Circle** the name of the friend that has **MORE** fruit and veggies.

Flora

Kit

Ocean Lengths

How long is each ocean animal? **Count** the number of blocks for each.

Cereal Count

Count the number of stars and hearts. **Write** each number in its square.

Hats Galore!

How many **different** types of hats do you see? Cross out the hats as you count.
Write the number in the box.

The Learnalots™

Counting Pairs

A pair is two of something. **Count** the animal pairs. **Write** the number of pairs in the circle.

Collection Counting

Write **down** the number of items in each collection.
On each page, **circle** the collection that has 2 more items than the other.

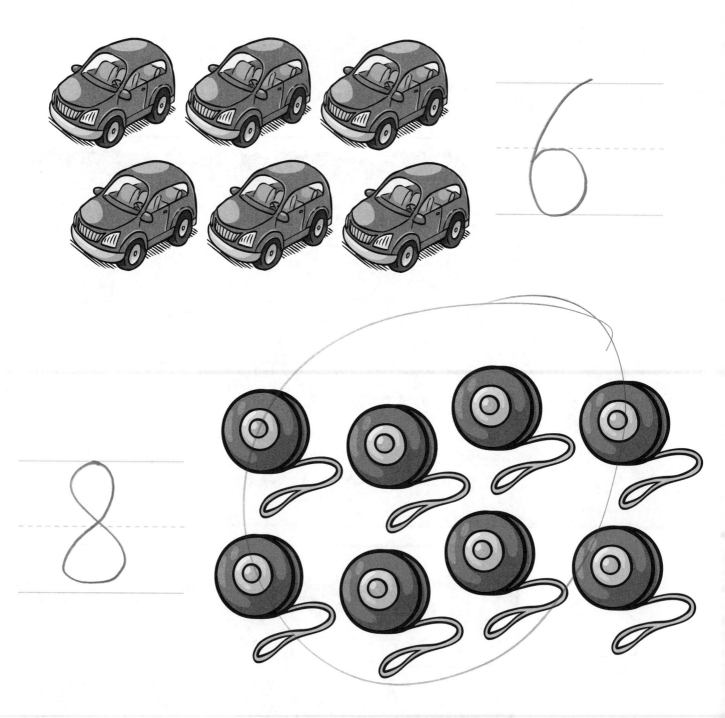

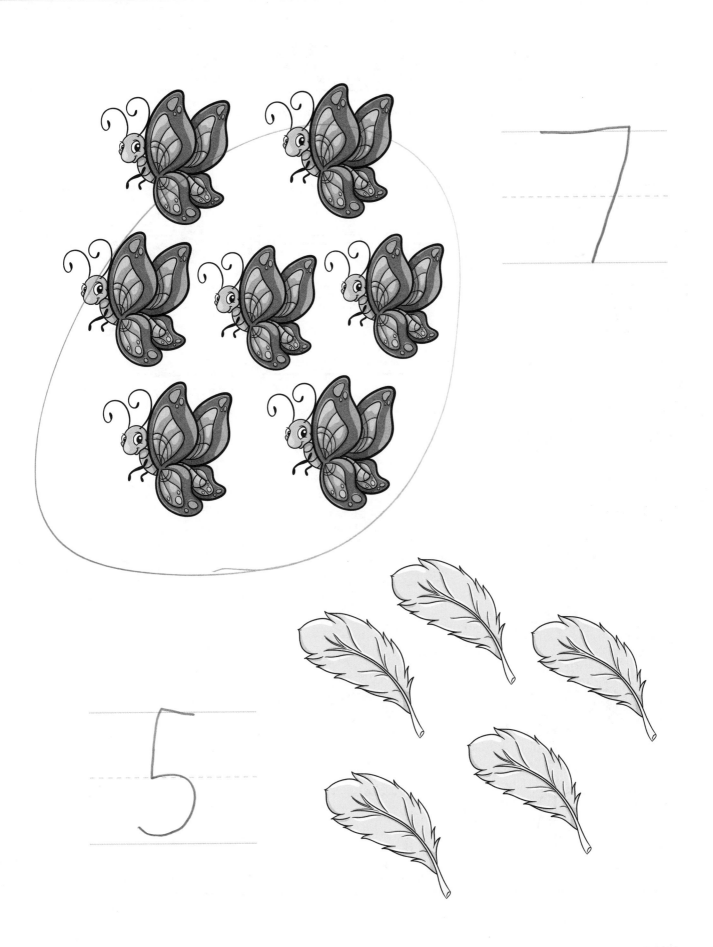

Counting Worms

Count how many worms each bird is about to eat. **Write** the number in each box.

The Learnalots

Two Hungry Mice

These hungry mice found a snack. **Connect the dots**, starting at 10, to find out what it is.

Snowboard Fun

Use these directions to **color** the snowboards.

Tallest = [ ] blue   Shortest = [ ] yellow   Widest = [ ] purple   Skinniest = [ ] red

The Learnalots

Beehive Directions

Draw a picture of a bee **over** the branch, **in** the hive, and **under** the hive.

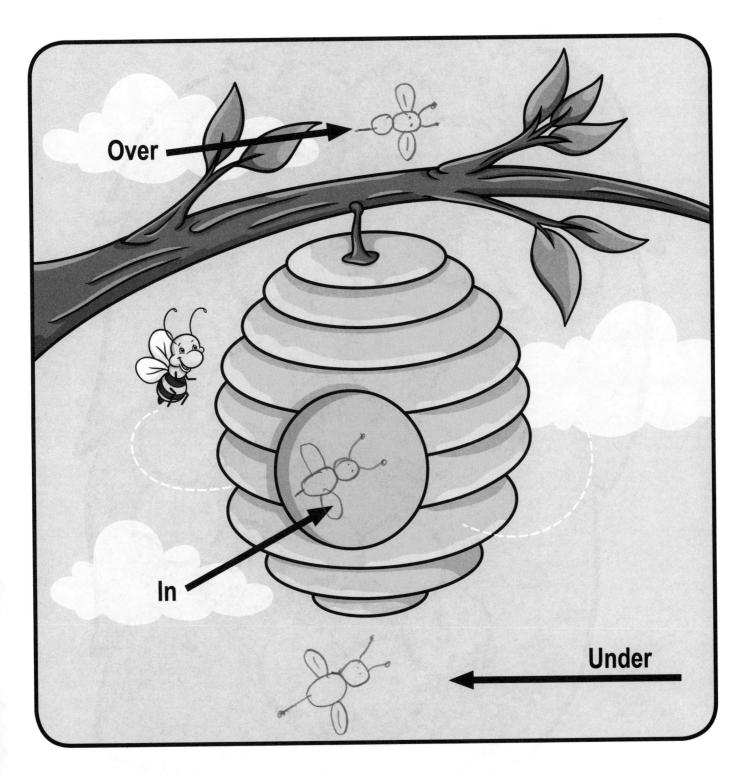

Follow the Numbers!

Fill in the blanks on the caterpillar's segments with the correct numbers in the sequence.

The Learnalots™

Numbers Maze

Follow the numbers in the correct order to help Kit **find** the beach.

Counting Pennies

Which items can Kit and Scout afford to buy? **Write down** the number of each friend's pennies.
Draw a line from each number to the item with the matching price.

Kit's pennies

¢

11¢

10¢

5¢

8¢

Scout's pennies

¢

The Learnalots

Kit's pennies

_____ ¢

13¢

6¢

7¢

12¢

Scout's pennies

_____ ¢

Birthday Math

Cross out one thing from each row and **count** how many are left.
Write the number in the circle.

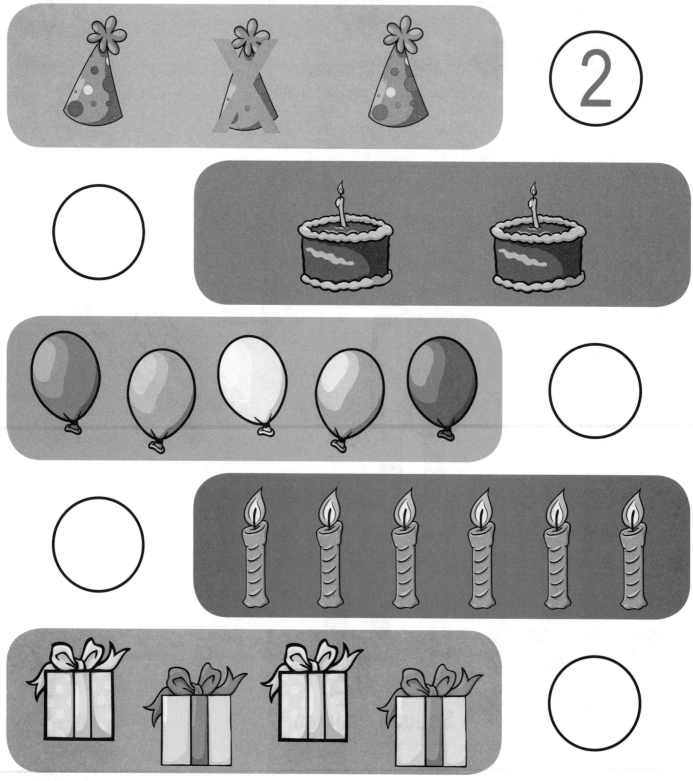

The Learnalots

What Time is It?

How many clocks show 6 o'clock? How many clocks show 10 o'clock?
Write your answers in the boxes.

6 o'clock

10 o'clock

Hungry Squirrel

How many acorns did the squirrel find? **Write** down your **guess**.
Then, **count** the acorns and **write** down the number.

Guess:

Count:

The Learnalots

Tic-Tac-Toe

Use the butterfly and train stickers
to **play tic-tac-toe** with a friend!
Three in a row wins!

Instrument Names

Trace the name of each instrument.

tuba

drum

lyre

The Learnalots™

chimes

flute

trumpet

Sounds of Music

We can make music by plucking, blowing, shaking, beating, and bowing instruments.
Draw a line to connect each instrument with the word that describes how you play it.

blow   beat   shake   bow   pluck

The Learnalots™

Scrambled Instrument

Piper is playing an instrument in this scrambled picture.
Circle the instrument you think she is playing.

String Instruments

String instruments have strings that are plucked or bowed.
Trace the name of each string instrument on the next page.
Then, **write** a number in each box to match the picture below to the name.

The Learnalots

Harp ☐

Violin ☐

Guitar ☐

Banjo ☐

Mismatched Percussion

Percussion instruments are played by hitting, rubbing, or scraping them.
Circle the instrument that is **not** in the percussion family.

triangle

flute

bongos

drum

cymbals

The Learnalots

Close-Up Instrument

Piper is looking close-up at an instrument. Which instrument do you think it could be?

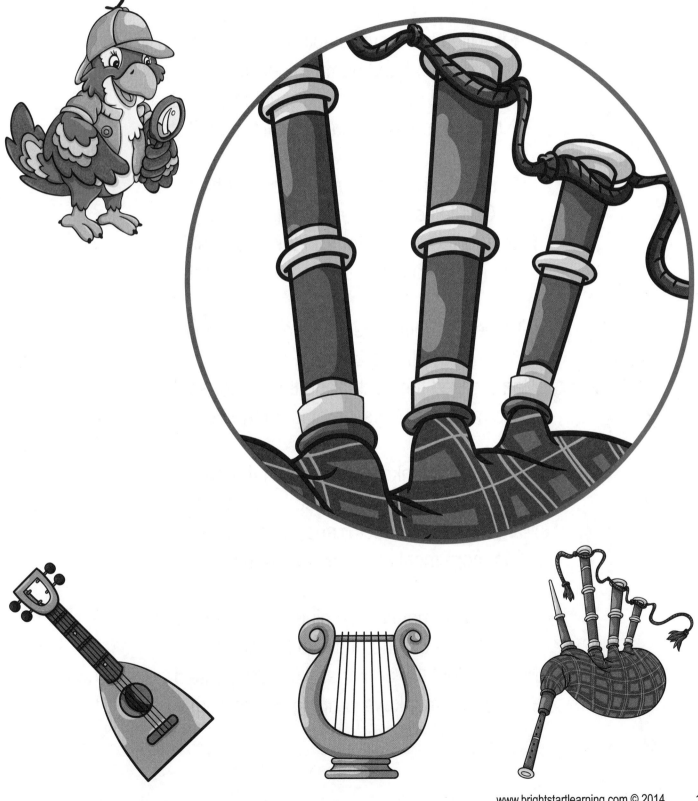

Five Little Monkeys

Sing the song and **color** the picture!

Five little monkeys jumping on the bed.
One fell off and bumped her head.
Mama called the doctor and the doctor said,
"No more monkeys jumping on the bed!"

Four little monkeys jumping on the bed.
One fell off and bumped his head.
Mama called the doctor and the doctor said,
"No more monkeys jumping on the bed!"

Three little monkeys jumping on the bed.
One fell off and bumped her head.
Mama called the doctor and the doctor said,
"No more monkeys jumping on the bed!"

Two little monkeys jumping on the bed.
One fell off and bumped his head.
Mama called the doctor and the doctor said,
"No more monkeys jumping on the bed!"

One little monkey jumping on the bed.
She fell off and bumped her head.
Mama called the doctor and the doctor said,
"No more monkeys jumping on the bed!"

The Learnalots

Steady Beat

Music can speed up, slow down, or have a steady beat.
Trace the word for the steady sound made by each object.

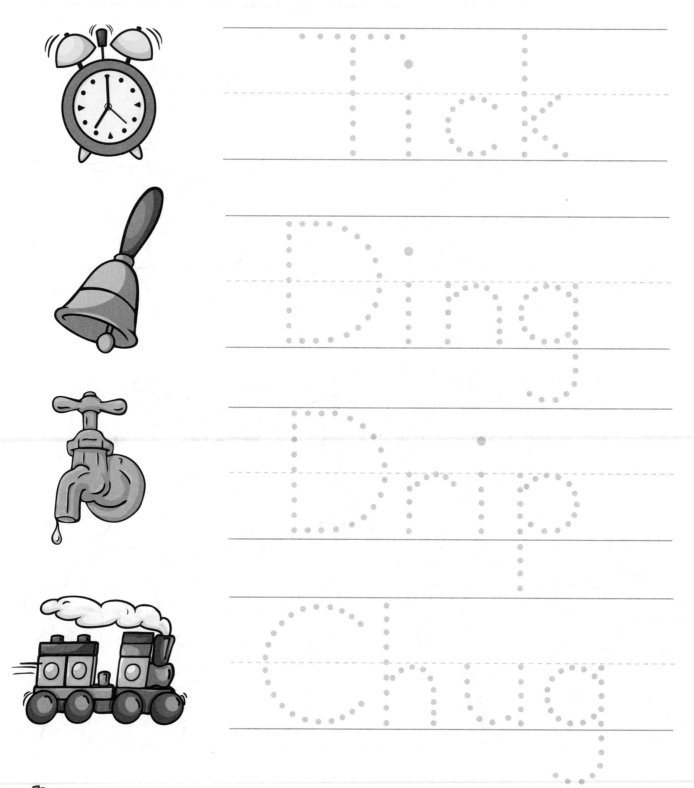

The Learnalots

Note Patterns

Finish the music patterns by **drawing** the note that comes next.

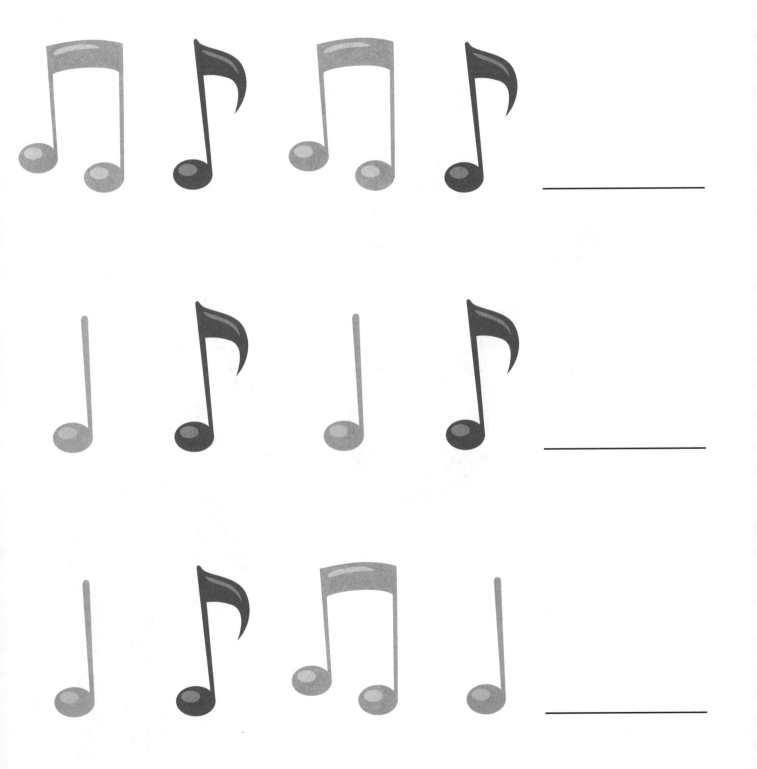

Shady Instruments

Draw a line to connect each instrument with its matching shadow.

The Learnalots

Connect the Dots

Connect the dots, 1-10. Color Piper's harp.

The Learnalots

Music Words

Circle the animal that goes with each sound word.

High or Low?

Circle the animal that is **HIGH**.

Fast or Slow?

Circle the animal that is **SLOW**.

Metal Music

Some musical instruments are made from metal. **Cross out** the instruments that are not made of metal.

The Learnalots

Go Rhythm Go!

Music has different beats. Some are short and some are long.
First, **write** a **S** on the short bars and a **L** on the long bars.
Then, **clap** the rhythms of short and long beats.

Short → S

Long → L

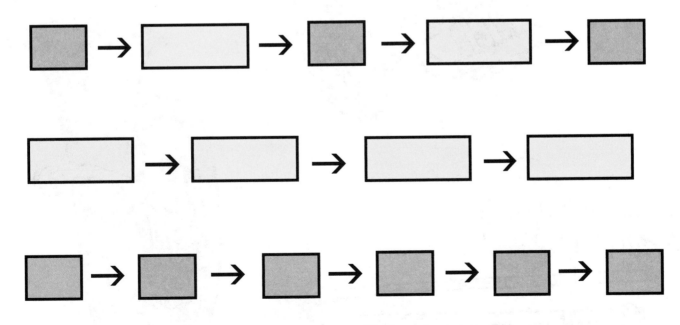

Pair of Instruments

Which two instruments are the same? **Circle** the matching pair.

The Learnalots™

Twinkle, Twinkle Little Star

Sing the song and **color** the picture!

Twinkle, twinkle, little star,
How I wonder what you are!
Up above the world so high,
Like a diamond in the sky!

Twinkle, twinkle, little star,
How I wonder what you are!

The Learnalots

Dressed for Dance

Piper loves to dance. She wears different shoes for each type of dance.
Draw a picture of your favorite type of dancing shoes.

Ballet

Square

Hip Hop

The Learnalots

Monster Mash

Add stickers to **finish** the faces of these dancing monsters.

Butterfly Story

Place the butterfly's life story in order. **Write 1** for what happens first.
Write 2 for what happens second. **Write 3** for what happens third.
Write 4 for what happens fourth.

The Learnalots

Young and Adult

Animals change as they grow. **Draw a line** to connect each young and adult pair.

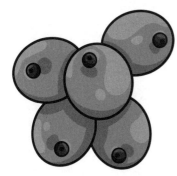

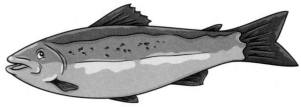

Name That Animal

Write these animal names by tracing each word.

moose

koala

lion

penguin

The Learnalots

So Many Feathers!

Draw a line to connect each bird to its feather.

ostrich

bluebird

goose

peacock

flamingo

Animal Groups

Animals are sorted into groups. **Trace** the name of the group to which each animal belongs.

elephant   wombat   bear

M a m m a l

salamander   frog   newt

A m p h i b i a n

velociraptor

snake

turtle

Reptile

Bird

goose

hummingbird

owl

shark

Fish

bass

angelfish

Furry Coats

Circle the animals that have fur.

cheetah

beaver

chick

frog

snake

deer

The Learnalots™

Animal Riddle

Circle the answer to this riddle:

I live in a bowl.
I love to swim.
My scales are golden.
Who am I?

Reptiles

Reptiles are a group of animals that lay eggs and have scales or plates. **Circle** the reptiles.

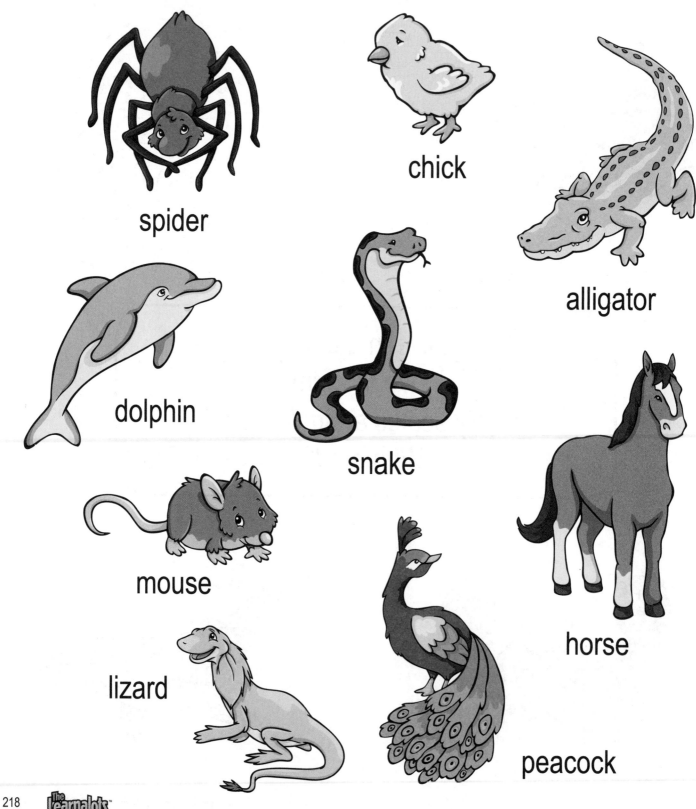

spider

chick

alligator

dolphin

snake

mouse

horse

lizard

peacock

The Learnalots

Four Leaf Clover

Can you **find** and **circle** the four-leaf clover? It's good luck!

Missing Tails

Draw a line to connect each animal and its missing tail.

The Learnalots

Natural Orders

Write the numbers **1, 2, 3, 4, and 5** to order the pictures.

Mammals

Mammals are a group of animals that have fur or hair and do not lay eggs. **Circle** the mammals.

bird

caterpillar

tiger

fish

shark

polar bear

dog

rabbit

The Learnalots

Animal Riddle

Circle the answer to this riddle:

I eat bugs.
I love the sun.
I can climb up walls.
Who am I?

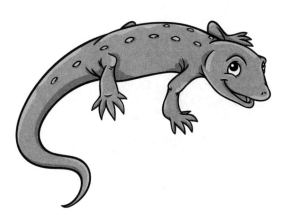

Autumn Leaves

In autumn, leaves change color before falling to the ground.
Write the numbers **1, 2, 3, 4, and 5** to order the leaves as they change from green to yellow.

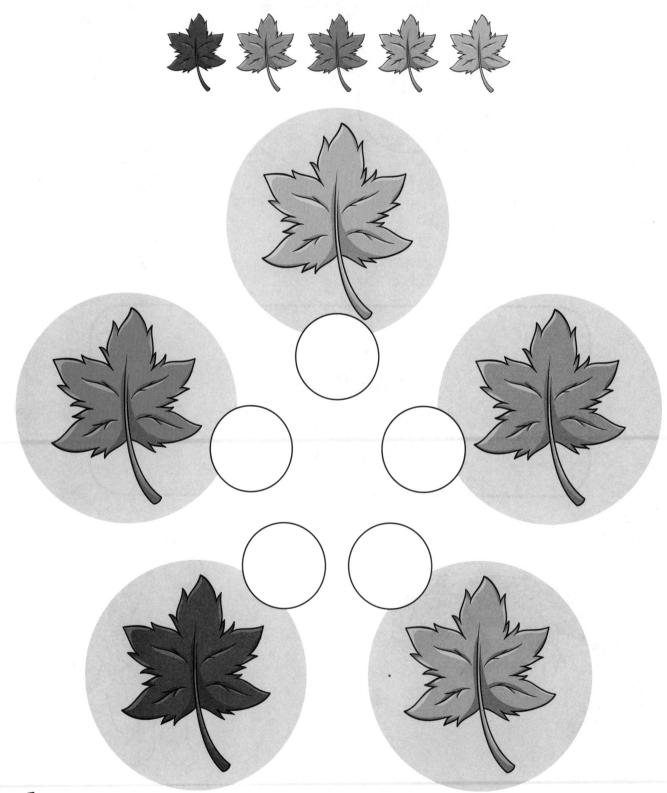

The Learnalots™

Recycling Day

Help sort the items that can be recycled. **Draw a line** to connect each item with its recycling bin.

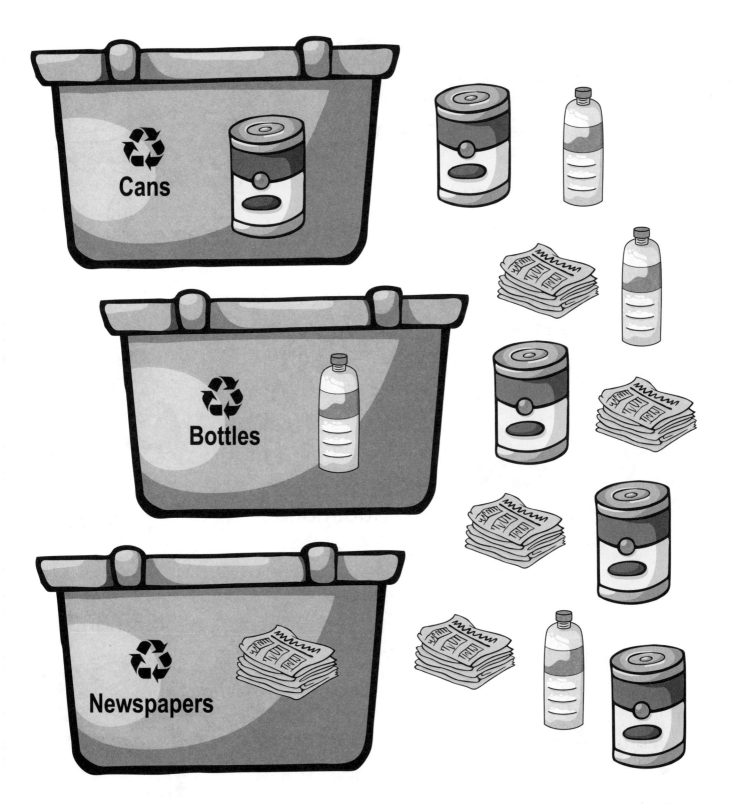

Amphibians

Amphibians are a group of animals that have moist skin. Mostly, they lay their eggs in water. They live in the water and on land. **Circle** the amphibians.

newt

tadpole

bat

dalmation

toad

bass

bee

salamander

frog

Learnalots

Whose Antler?

Some animals grow and shed antlers each year. Flora found this antler in the forest.
Circle the animal that goes with this antler.

moose

elk

deer

Underground Animals

Circle the animals that tunnel or burrow underground.

cow

worm

groundhog

bear

bird

rabbit

crab

gopher

The Learnalots

Little Leaves

Circle the two leaves in each row that match.

Birds

Birds are a group of animals that have feathers and wings and lay eggs. **Circle** the birds.

eagle

toucan

butterfly

beaver

chicken

ant

turkey

peacock

hedgehog

The Learnalots™

Shell Search

Circle the animals that have shells.

turtle

fox

rabbit

armadillo

hermit crab

pig

deer

snail

Octopus Tangle

Find the arm that caught the pearl necklace and **trace** it back to the octopus's body. How many arms does the octopus have?

The Learnalots™

Ocean or Land?

Circle the items that came from the ocean.

Feathered Friends

Circle the animals that have feathers.

owl

dog

hummingbird

mouse

turtle

turkey

Animal Names

Find the animal sticker that matches each animal name.

alligator

bear

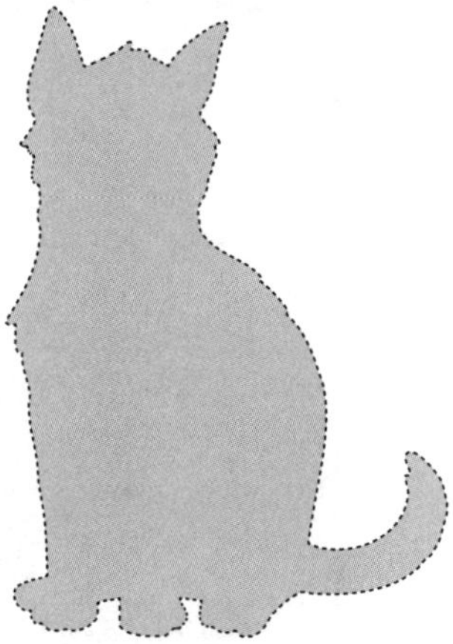

cat

jaguar

fox

giraffe

rabbit

Mountain Slopes

Swoosh! Scout is learning to ski.
Circle the objects that don't belong on the mountain slope.

The Learnalots

Snow Sports

Circle the objects that are used in winter sports.

Sunny Days

Circle the items that protect you from the sun.

The Learnalots

Picture Punt

Use these directions to **find** the hidden picture.

1 = brown   **2** = yellow   **3** = blue   **4** = green

Splash Sports!

Some sports are played in water and others on dry land. **Circle** the sports that are played in water. Then **draw a line** between water sports and the ocean.

The Learnalots™

Snorkeling Scout

Connect the dots, 1-21, to find out who is swimming with Scout.

Tennis Time

Circle the things you need to play tennis.

The Learnalots

Sports Maze

Follow the path with only sports objects.

Helmet Sports

Circle the activities that you need a helmet to play.

Rise and Shine

Good morning! Scout eats healthy breakfast foods to help him grow big and strong.
Circle the healthy foods. **Cross out** the unhealthy foods.

Healthy	Not Healthy
• Milk	• Cupcake
• Eggs	• Milkshake
• Cereal	• Pie
• Yogurt	
• Toast	

MILK

Hidden Picture Picnic

Find the hidden pictures in the picnic scene below.

The Learnalots

Slurp!

Circle the foods that make a slurpy sound when you eat them.

Veggie Colors

Which is the correct color for each vegetable? **Color** the veggies!

pepper

corn

The Learnalots™

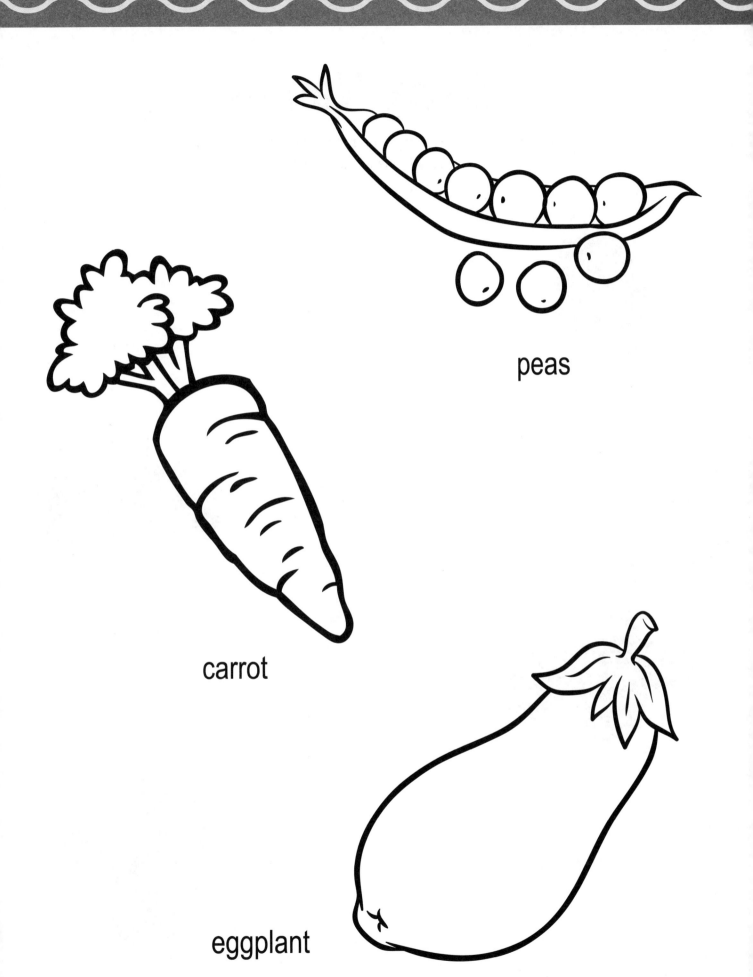

peas

carrot

eggplant

Berry Names

Berries are a delicious type of fruit. **Trace** the name of each kind of berry.
Which one is your favorite?

strawberry

raspberry

blackberry

cranberry

The **Learnalots**™

Delicious Dairy

Draw a line to connect the cow and the dairy foods that are made from her milk.

Tasty Tic-Tac-Toe

Play tic-tac-toe with a friend. Take turns **drawing** apples and bananas. Three in a row wins!

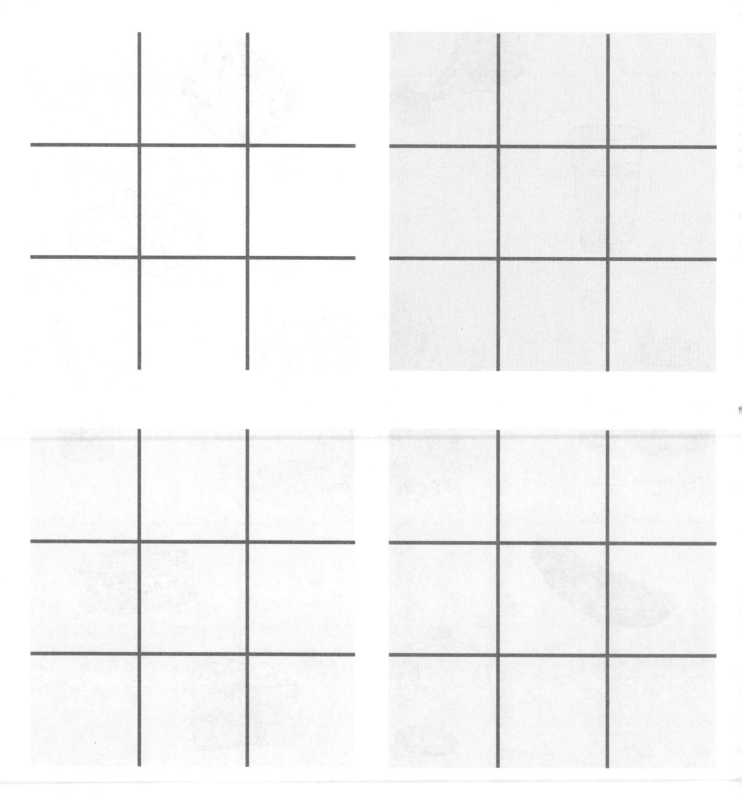

The Learnalots

Hot or Cold?

Some foods are eaten cold and others hot.
Draw a **circle** around the hot foods and **draw** a **square** around the cold foods.

Five Senses

What are your five senses? Practice **tracing** each word

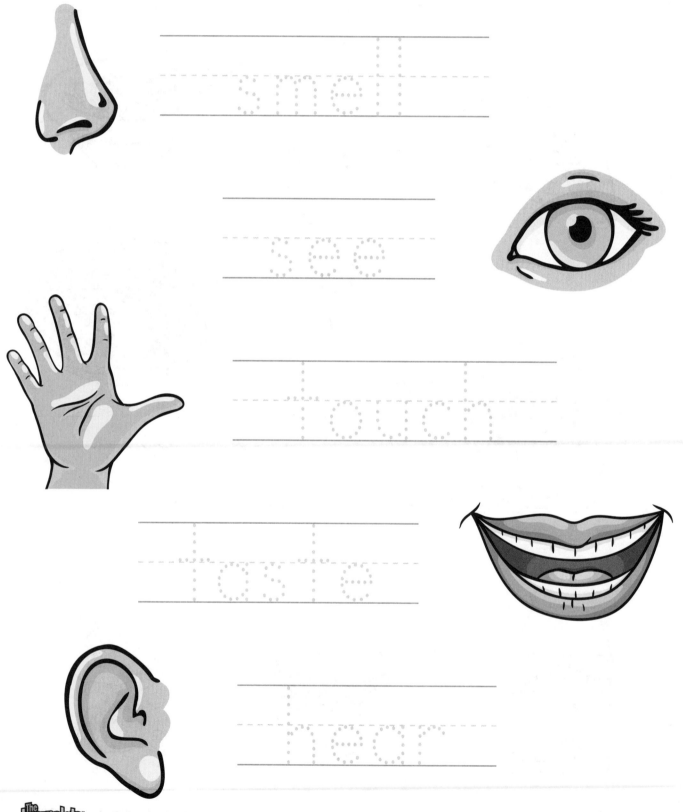

smell

see

touch

taste

hear

The Learnalots

Hair Wash

Put these steps in order for washing your hair. **Write** the numbers **1, 2, 3, and 4** to order the pictures.

Learnalots Puzzle

Add the **puzzle stickers** to finish the puzzle.

The Learnalots

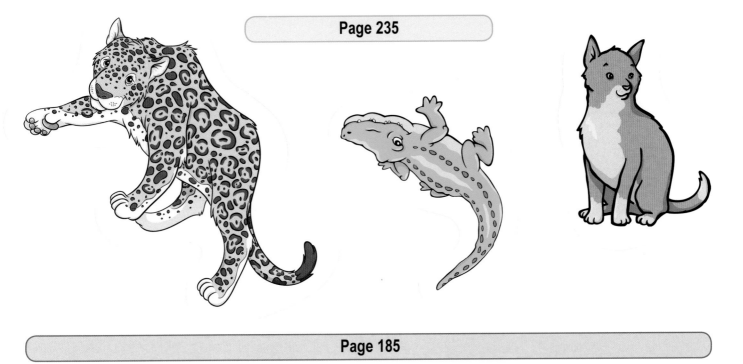